MacFarlane

by Jim Hewitson

LangSyne
PUBLISHING
WRITING *to* REMEMBER

LangSyne
PUBLISHING
WRITING *to* REMEMBER

79 Main Street, Newtongrange,
Midlothian EH22 4NA
Tel: 0131 344 0414   Fax: 0845 075 6085
E-mail: info@lang-syne.co.uk
www.langsyneshop.co.uk

Design by Dorothy Meikle
Printed by Ricoh Print Scotland
© Lang Syne Publishers Ltd 2015

ISBN 978-1-85217-070-7

Macfarlane

SEPT NAMES INCLUDE:

Allen	MacRobb
Bartholomew	MacWalter
Bartlett	MacWilliam
Bryce	Miller
Callander	Napier
Galbraith	Parlane
Galloway	Robb
Lennox	Smith
MacAllan	Sproul
MacGeoch	Stalker
MacGurk	Thomason
MacInally	Weaver
MacKinlay	Webster
MacNair	Weir
MacParland	Williamson
MacParlane	Wylie

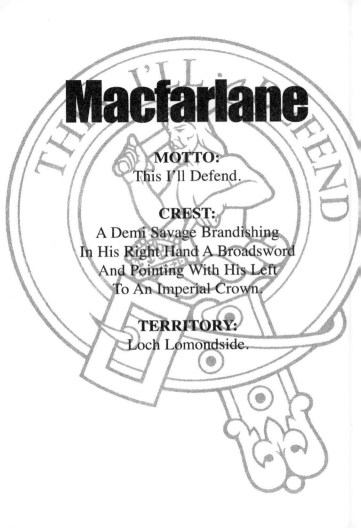

Macfarlane

MOTTO:
This I'll Defend.

CREST:
A Demi Savage Brandishing
In His Right Hand A Broadsword
And Pointing With His Left
To An Imperial Crown.

TERRITORY:
Loch Lomondside.

Chapter one:

The origins of the clan system

by Rennie McOwan

The original Scottish clans of the Highlands and the great families of the Lowlands and Borders were gatherings of families, relatives, allies and neighbours for mutual protection against rivals or invaders.

Scotland experienced invasion from the Vikings, the Romans and English armies from the south. The Norman invasion of what is now England also had an influence on land-holding in Scotland. Some of these invaders stayed on and in time became 'Scottish'.

The word clan derives from the Gaelic language term 'clann', meaning children, and it was first used many centuries ago as communities were formed around tribal lands in glens and mountain fastnesses.

The format of clans changed over the centuries, but at its best the chief and his family held the land on behalf of all, like trustees, and the ordinary clansmen and women believed they had a blood relationship with the founder of their clan.

There were two way duties and obligations. An inadequate chief could be deposed and replaced by someone of greater ability.

Clan people had an immense pride in race. Their relationship with the chief was like adult children to a father and they had a real dignity.

The concept of clanship is very old and a more feudal notion of authority gradually crept in.

Pictland, for instance, was divided into seven principalities ruled by feudal leaders who were the strongest and most charismatic leaders of their particular groups.

By the sixth century the 'British' kingdoms of Strathclyde, Lothian and Celtic Dalriada (Argyll) had emerged and Scotland, as one nation, began to take shape in the time of King Kenneth MacAlpin.

Some chiefs claimed descent from

ancient kings which may not have been accurate in every case.

By the twelfth and thirteenth centuries the clans and families were more strongly brought under the central control of Scottish monarchs.

Lands were awarded and administered more and more under royal favour, yet the power of the area clan chiefs was still very great.

The long wars to ensure Scotland's independence against the expansionist ideas of English monarchs extended the influence of some clans and reduced the lands of others.

Those who supported Scotland's greatest king, Robert the Bruce, were awarded the territories of the families who had opposed his claim to the Scottish throne.

In the Scottish Borders country – the notorious Debatable Lands – the great families built up a ferocious reputation for providing warlike men accustomed to raiding into England and occasionally fighting one another.

Chiefs had the power to dispense justice and to confiscate lands and clan warfare produced a society where martial virtues – courage, hardiness, tenacity – were greatly admired.

Gradually the relationship between the clans and the Crown became strained as Scottish monarchs became more orientated to life in the Lowlands and, on occasion, towards England.

The Highland clans spoke a different language, Gaelic, whereas the language of Lowland Scotland and the court was Scots and in more modern times, English.

Highlanders dressed differently, had different customs, and their wild mountain land sometimes seemed almost foreign to people living in the Lowlands.

It must be emphasised that Gaelic culture was very rich and story-telling, poetry, piping, the clarsach (harp) and other music all flourished and were greatly respected.

Highland culture was different from other parts of Scotland but it was not inferior or less sophisticated.

Central Government, whether in London or Edinburgh, sometimes saw the Gaelic clans as

*"The spirit of the clan means much
to thousands of people"*

a challenge to their authority and some sent expeditions into the Highlands and west to crush the power of the Lords of the Isles.

Nevertheless, when the eighteenth century Jacobite Risings came along the cause of the Stuarts was mainly supported by Highland clans.

The word Jacobite comes from the Latin for James – Jacobus. The Jacobites wanted to restore the exiled Stuarts to the throne of Britain.

The monarchies of Scotland and England became one in 1603 when King James VI of Scotland (1st of England) gained the English throne after Queen Elizabeth died.

The Union of Parliaments of Scotland and England, the Treaty of Union, took place in 1707.

Some Highland clans, of course, and Lowland families opposed the Jacobites and supported the incoming Hanoverians.

After the Jacobite cause finally went down at Culloden in 1746 a kind of ethnic cleansing took place. The power of the chiefs was curtailed. Tartan and the pipes were banned in law.

Many emigrated, some because they

wanted to, some because they were evicted by force. In addition, many Highlanders left for the cities of the south to seek work.

Many of the clan lands became home to sheep and deer shooting estates.

But the warlike traditions of the clans and the great Lowland and Border families lived on, with their descendants fighting bravely for freedom in two world wars.

Remember the men from whence you came, says the Gaelic proverb, and to that could be added the role of many heroic women.

The spirit of the clan, of having roots, whether Highland or Lowland, means much to thousands of people.

A map of the clans' homelands

Chapter two:

Written in blood

Landscape has always played a vital role in Scotland's unfolding history, from the time when the Roman legions tramped the glens of Perthshire and earlier invaders halted and took stock at the various gateways to the Highlands ranged along the boundary fault line. They were fully aware that through the mists, at the top of the glens, lay a new and dangerous domain.

The Guardians of these strategic natural portals have always figured prominently in the tempestuous annals of Scotland and in the case of the Clan Macfarlane, accepted as one of the oldest and most warlike of the warrior clans, their history is indeed often written in blood.

From the West Highlands one of the principal routes leading to the conspicuously fertile and more densely populated Central Lowlands crosses a narrow neck of land from

Loch Long (a sea loch giving access to the Clyde estuary) to Loch Lomond. This is the strip of land – hardly more than a mile wide – across which the Vikings once, famously, dragged their longships to plunder the rich agricultural community which had developed on the islands and along Loch Lomondside and its hinterland. This is also the territory of the Macfarlanes.

The Macfarlanes were cattle thieves of some repute and their hideaways were high among

the waterfalls and glens surrounding Loch Sloy, an inaccessible spot where they drove herds and flocks several hundred strong into remote corries.

The clan adopted the name of the loch as their battle cry, or as the more genteel might have it, the clan motto. But in the 1500s and 1600s it was a phrase which often struck terror into the hearts of their many enemies.

Although Loch Sloy, right in the heart of Macfarlane country, is enlarged as a result of the ambitious hydro-electric scheme, it was still ideal for herding cattle into the high corries, out of reach of their rivals. Appropriately the tune played on the bagpipe for the clan gathering was Thogail nam bo – Lifting the Cattle.

With good reason the Macfarlanes were known through West Central Scotland as "the Wild Ones" with the bracken and scree covered sloped and empty glens in the vicinity of Arrochar as their stomping ground. One noted Lowlander, Robert Burns no less, was moved to classify the weather, the land, the sheep and most of all the people in this vicinity as 'savage'.

Chapter three:

Macfarlanes' lantern

The Macfarlanes were a cadet branch of the old Celtic Earls of Lennox, a family which played a pivotal role in the power politics of Scotland for many hundreds of years. Officially the Macfarlanes were of the line of Gilchrist, a younger brother of the Third Earl of Lennox (Maldouen), having been granted the lands around Arrochar from his big brother. Later Macfarlane chiefs were in no doubt that they were the true representatives of that 'great and ancient family'.

In fact, the clan took its name in the 14th century from Gilchrist's great-grandson Parlan, the Gaelic form of Bartholomew, a staunch supporter of Robert Bruce.

In the Lennox area which stretched away to the east towards Glasgow and into Stirlingshire, the populations were partly agricultural and trading while others – like the Macfarlanes – were

predatory and warlike. These were troubled and
unsettled times and naturally there was conflict.

One of the earliest recorded episodes of
strife involving the Macfarlanes which is
found in any detail was an incident in 1515
commemorated in his poem 'Squyer Meldrum'
by Sir David Lindsay. Marion Lawson, widow of
John Haldane of Gleneagles, while in residence at
her castle of Strathearn, received news that her
lands around Boturich on Loch Lomondside were
being harried by the Macfarlanes. In the opening
stanzas we learn:

Ane messenger come speedily,
From the Lennox to his ladie,
Schewing how that Macfarlane,
And with him many bauld barons,
Her castell had tane perfors,
And neither left her kow nor hors…

Her lover, Squire Meldrum, chivalrous
gent that he was, at once undertook the recovery
of her property which the poet describes him
accomplishing amid circumstances of unparalleled
bravery. The Macfarlanes had actually taken

possession of the tower of Boturich which Meldrum attacked and carried, Andrew Macfarlane, the chief, making unconditional surrender.

A bit of a humiliation for the Macfarlanes but glory days all the way for Meldrum who we are told by Lindsay:

> *Syne to Strathearn returnit again,*
> *quhair that he*
> *By his fair ladie ressavit was full*
> *pleasantlie.*

Inevitably as kinsmen and supporters of the Stewart Earls of Lennox they had been drawn increasingly during the 14th and 15th centuries into the nation's often confused and bloodthirsty affairs. They also saw themselves in the role of protectors of the fertile lands against bands of Highland 'caterans', bloodthirsty marauders who came spilling down the glens seeking easy pickings on the rolling lands beyond Loch Lomond.

Although on the clan shield you'll find the declaration – 'This I'll Defend' it was not in the nature of the Macfarlanes to indulge in purely

containing measures and around this time they
went into an expansionist phase, extending their
sphere of influence to the head of Loch Lomond
and into Perthshire.

They roamed this territory offering protection to home and herd for cash (the origin of blackmail from black meal) and if this offer failed to impress, a torched croft and an empty cattle enclosure was the likely conclusion to negotiations. This was also the period when a moon, thought favourable for staging a cattle raid, became known, far beyond the confines of the clan lands, as 'Macfarlanes' Lantern'.

For example, in May, 1543, the Macfarlanes organised a raid on Garelochhead and carried off from Faslane and Little Balernock, 280 head of cattle, 80 sheep, 24 goats, 20 horses and mares, 80 stones of cheese and 40 bolls of barley besides murdering some of the unfortunate people.

In the following year with a motley crew of 600 'great thieves, limmers, robbers, common sorners of the lieges, throat-cutters, murderers, slayers of men, wives and bairns' they harried the Colquhoun country, murdering nine of the tenants in their beds and setting the scene for even more gory events around the turn of the century.

Chapter four:

Slings and arrows

Macfarlanes were skilled with the bow and arrow. This talent was honed among the bracken covered hills in search of deer and for the young Macfarlane boys the skills of the hunter were as important as walking and breathing.

In fact, the Macfarlane's record of service to the Scottish throne is an impressive one and compares favourably with that of any other clan. Among those who gave their lives in defence of the Scottish establishment during the medieval period were clan chiefs Walter (Sauchieburn, 1488); Sir Iain Macfarlane (Flodden, 1513) and Duncan Macfarlane (Pinkie, 1547).

However, when Henry VIII was stirring up trouble during the childhood of Mary Queen of Scots, trying to secure a marriage contract between his son Edward and Mary by force of arms (the so-called Rough Wooing), we find the

Macfarlanes ranged with the English King as supporters of the Protestant cause.

When Henry landed at Dumbarton, the chronicler Holinshead tells us that Walter Macfarlane of Tarbet brought a force of 140 men, well-armoured and carrying bows in the traditional Macfarlane style, as well as two handed swords, to join Henry's forces.

As we've seen Duncan Macfarlane died at Pinkie but it was his son Andrew who is judged by history to have been the most enthusiastic supporter of the Reformation cause illustrated by the pivotal, if enigmatic, role played by the Macfarlanes in the battle of Langside (1568). This brief but bloody encounter on the outskirts of Glasgow saw the end of Mary's cause in Scotland and forced her flight to imprisonment and eventual execution in England.

At Langside the Macfarlanes are cast as heroes by some, villians by others.

For the Queen, the Hamiltons led the charge but were soon locked in a violent duel with the Border pikemen under Moray. The two forces

pushed and sweated for fully half-an-hour, their
pikes locked together.

At one point, say the histories, the
Macfarlanes and their chief fled from the position
on the battlefield assigned to them by the Regent.
Their place was occupied by the forces of Lord
Lindsay who, according to folklore, is said to have
shouted after them: *'Let them go, I shall fill up
their place better myself'*.

Reasons for the Macfarlane withdrawal
are unclear. However, the timing of their return to
the fray was immaculate. The Regent's forces had
broken the Queen's ranks and the Macfarlanes
rejoined the action and as one historian has
commented: *'in the pursuit of the enemy, the
Macfarlanes showed an activity that made
amends for their former cowardice'*.

Around this time we also learn that the
Clan Macfarlane was in cahoots, or at least in
neighbours by the loch, Clan Gregor. Together
they pursued a vendetta against the Colquhouns of
Luss which ended in murder and mayhem. It
seems that toward the end of the 16th century

Dunbartonshire was torn by cross feuds and personal vendettas which stain the history of the country.

The murder of Sir Humphrey Colquhoun at his castle of Bannachra in Glen Fruin was an atrocious affair. Apparently Andrew Macfarlane's wife had been, in the terminology of the time, dallying with Sir Humphrey and when the Macfarlanes cornered and butchered the knight they are also said to have raped his daughter Jean, murdered his servants and laid waste to the lands of Luss. Almost par for the course in those days, there also seems to have been some treachery in the Colquhoun household.

Also in keeping with the violent and degrading times legend has it that the wayward wife of the Macfarlane chief then had her lover's genitals served up to her as sweetmeats.

By 1594, along with the infamous MacGregors, the Macfarlanes were listed among the broken clans and were the subject of official repression.

The Valley of the Fruin, or Glen of

Sorrows, lies between Loch Lomond and Loch Long and is a lonely, haunted place at the best of times. At the head of the valley near the farmstead of Strone the feud between the Colquhouns and the MacGregors and their Macfarlane allies reached a bloody watershed in February, 1603, when Alastair MacGregor of Glenstrae overwhelmed a force led by Alexander Colquhoun of Luss. The defeated contingent, which included well-meaning burgesses from Dumbarton, was pursued to the gates of the Colquhoun stronghold at Rossdhu on Loch Lomond, stragglers being slaughtered as they were overtaken.

It's said that a party of schoolboys who had come from Dumbarton to watch the battle were murdered by MacGregors.

As the full force of the law turned on the MacGregors – twenty-five were executed for their part in the Glen Fruin affair – the Macfarlanes, father Andrew and son John, saw the way the wind was blowing and turned on their former allies, helping to hunt them down while at the same time winning back official favour.

Chapter five:

Changing times

**Events had turned full circle on the religious
front in the middle of the 17th century. In
contrast with Andrew Macfarlane, 'hero' of
Langside and fervent supporter of the
Reformation, Walter then clan chief under
Charles I and II was at most a token
Covenanter and eventually declared himself
fully behind the Royalist cause. For his trouble,
his island castle near Inveruglas was destroyed
by the forces of Oliver Cromwell during the
occupation of Scotland during 1651.**

By the time of the Revolution in 1689
when the Scottish Convention declared that James
VII had forfeited the crown and offered it to
William of Orange and his wife Mary, the
Macfarlanes were well and truly back in the
Presbyterian camp.

On the social and business front towards
the end of the 1600s, the clan had a new seat, a

'handsome house with pleasure gardens' and
unlike the other Highland clans, the Macfarlanes
took an interest in the ambitious Darien Scheme
to establish a Scottish colony in Central America.
In fact, they subscribed to the expedition which
received its support mainly from the Lowland
Scots but as history tells us this ambitious
adventure was doomed to failure in the humidity
of the Panamanian jungle.

True to form, the clan supported the
Hanoverian succession from 1714 onwards.

Chroniclers have noted the activities of a
couple of intriguing Macfarlanes in the Lennox in
those first years of the 18th century. Robert
Macfarlane was minister of Buchanan on the east
side of Loch Lomond in 1720 and was suspended
by the Presbytery of Dumbarton for a month after
being accused of falling asleep by the ingle of a
roadside inn.

He pleaded pressure of work having just
completed three exhausting days of preaching.

At the '45 Uprising the Macfarlanes
stayed at home as Prince Charlie and his loyal

clans undertook the epic march to Derby and back to the bloody conclusion at Culloden.

A Duncan Macfarlane, minister at Drymen as well as factor at Arrochar chased off a band of caterans who filtered south from Sunart seeking to take advantage of the confusion in the immediate aftermath of the '45. This was one of the last such raids in the annals of the Western Highlands.

Duncan was a true soldier of the Lord and was known to have carried a cosh – which he was prepared to use – in order to still disputes of a more worldly kind.

During the 1700s the clan kept their heads well and truly below the parapet politically and this studied and cautious approach to life is best illustrated by Walter Macfarlane, student of antiquities whose attributes, according to one biographer, were 'a zest for a good pedigree, an intense love of Scotland and a jackdaw-like inquisitiveness'.

At the other end of the social scale and into the 19th century we encounter James

Mcfarlan (1832-1862), a pedlar poet, who walked from Glasgow to London in an effort to have a volume of his lyrics published in 1853; other volumes followed.

This was a time of change. On to the Macfarlane lands from the south came lowland farmers without any clan connections but who knew how to make best use of the land; they received a cool reception initially, but this development and the aftermath of Culloden had signalled the end of the old ways where everyone in the neighbourhood was generally a blood relation and owed allegiance and duty to the laird as hereditary chieftain. These newcomers were instead privately enterprising.

Mounting debts forced the sale of the clan estates in 1785. Legend had it that when a black swan appeared among the Macfarlane flock on Loch Lomond the chief would lose everything. Such a swan did appear just before the 23rd chief sold up and moved on to the United States.

While the military character of the Macfarlanes saw them serve in good numbers in the creation of the British Empire, new horizons were opening up for the clan through immigration. Many were pushed to a new life overseas by improvements on the land and disintegrating clan system and pulled by the prospect of becoming lords of the land in their own right and perhaps making a fortune on the vast pastures and goldfields of America, Canada, Australia and New Zealand.

Of course, among the Scots who took off to the young countries there was a keen desire to cherish their Scottish heritage and the Macfarlanes were no exception. Societies and groups taking the clan name sprang up all over the world, celebrating the Macfarlane heritage and open to anyone with the surname in any of its various spellings and to anyone with the surname of the 40 septs associated with the clan, including Allen, MacAllan, Miller, Napier, Weaver and Weir.